WEST : FIRE : ARCHIVE

The Mountain West Poetry Series
Stephanie G'Schwind, Donald Revell, Kazim Ali,
Dan Beachy-Quick & Camille T. Dungy, series editors

We Are Starved, by Joshua Kryah
The City She Was, by Carmen Giménez Smith
Upper Level Disturbances, by Kevin Goodan
The Two Standards, by Heather Winterer
Blue Heron, by Elizabeth Robinson
Hungry Moon, by Henrietta Goodman
The Logan Notebooks, by Rebecca Lindenberg
Songs, by Derek Henderson
The Verging Cities, by Natalie Scenters-Zapico
A Lamp Brighter than Foxfire, by Andrew S. Nicholson
House of Sugar, House of Stone, by Emily Pérez
&luckier, by Christopher J Johnson
Escape Velocity, by Bonnie Arning
We Remain Traditional, by Sylvia Chan
The Lapidary's Nosegay, by Lara Candland
Furthest Ecology, by Adam Fagin
The Minuses, by Jami Macarty
Dears, Beloveds, by Kevin Phan
West : Fire : Archive, by Iris Jamahl Dunkle

WEST : FIRE : ARCHIVE

POEMS

Iris Jamahl Dunkle

The Center for Literary Publishing
Colorado State University

For information about permission to reproduce
selections from this book, write to
The Center for Literary Publishing
attn: Permissions
9105 Campus Delivery
Colorado State University
Fort Collins, Colorado 80523-9105.

Printed in the United States of America.

Library of Congress Cataloging-in-Publication Data

Names: Dunkle, Iris Jamahl, author.
Title: West, fire, archive : poems / Iris Jamahl Dunkle.
Other titles: Mountain west poetry series.
Description: Fort Collins, Colorado : The Center for Literary Publishing,
Colorado State University, [2021] | Series: The mountain west poetry
series | Title appears on the title page with each word separated by a
space-colon-space. Commas added for clarity. | Includes bibliographical references.
Identifiers: LCCN 2020048140 (print) | LCCN 2020048141 (ebook)
ISBN 9781885635778 (paperback) | ISBN 9781885635785 (ebook)
Subjects: LCSH: London, Charmian--Poetry. | London, Jack,
1876-1916--Poetry. | Dunkle, Iris Jamahl--Poetry. | West (U.S.)--Poetry.
Classification: LCC PS3604.U5455 W47 2021 (print) | LCC PS3604.U5455
(ebook) | DDC 811/.6--dc23
LC record available at https://lccn.loc.gov/2020048140
LC ebook record available at https://lccn.loc.gov/2020048141

The paper used in this book meets the minimum requirements of the
American National Standard for Information Sciences-Permanence of Paper
for Printed Library Materials, ANSI Z39.48-1984.

Publication of this book was made possible by a generous grant
from the National Endowment for the Arts.

ART WORKS.

**National
Endowment
for the Arts**
arts.gov

To live past the end of your myth is a perilous thing.
—Anne Carson

CONTENTS

Box 1: Biography

Box 2: Autobiography

Box 3: Recorded History

Box 1: Biography

When you get lost on the road
You run into the dead

—Frank Stanford

Contents

Description
The forgotten moments from the life of Charmian Kittredge London (1871–1955). She was free-spirited, adventurous, and she defied gender norms. Today she is best known as the wife of the famous American author Jack London, yet she was a literary trailblazer in her own right.

Places
Racine, Wisconsin
A wagon train
Mount Desert Island, Maine
The gold fields of Mokelumne
Salt Lake City, Utah
Wilmington, California
San Francisco before 1906
San Francisco after 1906
Oakland, California
Glen Ellen, California
The *Snark*, a small yacht in the South Seas
The *Dirigo*, a schooner that sailed around Cape Horn

Documents
Personal diaries 1900–45
The *Dirigo* diaries, typed and retyped
The Log of the Snark
Our Hawaii
The Book of Jack London
Our Hawaii: Islands and Islanders

People
Charmian Kittredge London
He/Him (the man she married)
Eliza (his stepsister)
Mother
Father

Listening to the Caryatids on the Palace of Fine Arts

The curve of roof echoes the roll of golden
coast hills solidified in travertine
marble. In front, the reflecting pool's eye,

where the dome—the city's past—floats, is split
by swans. Once a city built from redwood
plank and gold dust, until earth shook it down

to mud and ash. In 1915, eleven
plaster palaces bloomed from the ruined
Marina. For nine months, San Francisco
grew fat again with visitors and fame.

The exhibition ends. Palaces razed.
Only this mute Roman structure remains,
crowned in weeping stone maidens who
whisper back to us in sea wind, bird song.

The Year He Was Born

At the 1876 World's Fair,
everything constructed
revealed the United States'
industrial prowess. Sky
above Philadelphia stitched tight
as a closed throat with coal dust.

And at the center hummed
the Corliss Engine: bulk of a house,
powering the blink and focus
of electric lights that flickered hope
up and down the midway

while underneath a city of unseen:
shoulders bent into shovels, coal-laced sweat,
ears echoing the scoop and drop
of mute black coal—

Sweatshop, Oakland, 1911

That the loss of a few fingers was normal
wear and tear. That the eyes got used to
the lack of light. That the skin paled,
became papery. That the sun ripped
open the day. That the soot never washed
out from under fingernails. That the back
never straightened again. That the fingers shook.
That the days lengthened after the earthquake.
Stitched closer and closer together by nervous
bosses. That the cracks were never filled. Grew wider.
That the sun strained to enter the greasy windows
until night broke it. That the irons singed.
That the beams ached every time a train
passed. That the girls looked up nervously to see
what others had done. That they fainted regularly.
That young girls of seven or eight were fastest.
That they secretly sang to each other under their breath.

Origin Story: Father, 1851–66

What's documented? Day of enlistment, promotion to captain.

Not the day he left his family and all he knew on the stone-jawed coast of Maine.

Not the long yawn of miles west that followed.

Or the sunset taste of wild strawberries on his tongue. The ones he'd found at the foot of a cottonwood after months of boiled beans in a cast-iron pot.

Not the way the prairie sea whispered to him at night.

Or how his body sank happily into the hard ground next to the star of another fire after days stretched out too long and too far.

Or how, when he arrived in the golden state, he spent hours hip-deep and tangled in the icy fingers of the creek seeking anything that shined.

Not the dust that rose from his horse's massive flanks, hooves cleaving the ground.

Not his company: a mass of brass buttons, blue cloth; tired men sheathed in seven-day beards, slumped on horseback; long road to another fort. This time on the thin lip of the Great Salt Lake.

Not even the swollen night at the dusty-floored dance when he met the young girl who could spill the universe from her black, curling hair—

Origin Story: Mother, 1870

By then, she's married the army captain and her family has gone west. By then, she knows two muddy ruts can lead to an un-diagrammable sentence.

The Wasatch Mountains rise, knuckled fists around her throat. Her husband, a bee stinging a map. Hold it to the right light and the lace makes a trail out.

By then, she's gone mute. Buried under her own blank diary pages. Time unfurls its magnolia-petal tongues until she leaves the city. Alone. Young girl looking at the cataracted eye of Salt Lake, from the window of the rocking stagecoach.

She tries to make sense of the change—from brackish water and taut sand bellies, to rise of sheer rock toward robin-blue sky.

Time moves molasses-slow.

For comfort, she cracks open a geology textbook, finds the story written on the land.

A long sentence that leads to scent of sage, cool silk of sand at dawn.

That leads to a long valley transformed into grassy hillsides, the rocky breath of sea.

Leads to her young brothers, grown large as men, her sisters knitting an Eden out of canvas tents—

The Curious Incident with the Horse, Charmian, Age 14

When we enter the scene, Charmian stands
in a doorway shadowed by the light. Her
mother has been dead from valley fever
eight years. Her father's body diminished:
no longer a decorated soldier,
parading on horseback over cobbled
streets. Now, he has become a shadow on
a borrowed cot. His blue fire put out.

It was a phaeton carriage that would
carry Charmian away from the sun's course,
from her father's pulse. From the dark house that
held him in its grasp. The horse's spun-silk
covered muscles. Foam frothing at its mouth.
Speed and wind beat her into a new self.

By the time she returned, his body had
been removed. She dropped the useless wax bag
filled with medicine she'd clutched in her hand.

Truth Walks the Plank, San Francisco, 1890–1900

At the edge of the packed ferry boat, water
and wind rush to erase her—

until out from veils of fog, land comes fast:
a clock-eyed ferry terminal, belted by boats,

and behind it sharpen the tiered rise of office
buildings, restaurants, homes: a city blinking

awake. It's a decade before the earth-
quake, before the fires satisfied their

ravenous appetites on anything
that tried to be a fact. When the boat docks,

Charmian walks the shaky plank between
then and now. Ash for water.

Lost papers fluttering. Hungry gulls calling—

Artifact

A whalebone corset: waist small enough to
fit between two circled hands. On nights when
stars pressed down and pinned their distance
Charmian wound those threaded bones around her own waist.

Her mother's manuscripts, written in
delicate ink, yellowing leaves of the cottonwoods
that come fall-raged red from the crags
of the Wasatch Mountains.

The tiny oval photo: her mother
posed in a bonnet, midnight curls falling
over her body as if to erase it.

The oval photograph hangs where no one
can see it. The manuscripts sealed in vaults.
Only scholars wearing white cotton gloves
can read them. The corset, wrapped in white tissue paper,
is stored in the dark mouth of Charmian's wooden dresser.

My mother has only been gone a few months
so I carry her artifacts in my purse.
A foldable hoof pick. A tiny wooden horse.
The gold ring I once bought her on a trip to Stockholm:
replica of one recovered from the *Vasa,*
an enormous ship found sunk, completely intact.
The weight of wood soaked and preserved by the clear harbor water.

After years of restoration, they dredged it up.
But the power and surge was gone.

Girl with a Gun Goes Anyway, Malaita, 1909

Each photograph opens a tiny portal.
In this one Charmian, wearing loose pants,
a revolver casually belted around her waist,
smiles amongst villagers at the women's market.

Face relaxed. Around her legs thick bandages cover mysterious sores.
Soon, the *Woman's Home Companion* will refuse to print the photograph,
claiming it obscene. Claiming the girl who smiles into adventure,
who wears pants and wields a gun is not woman-like.
Claiming a woman is too delicate to be so many months at sea.

Already the sea had exhaled her. Their boat had been belly
to belly with machete-scarred blackbirding ships.

Already, she'd witnessed plantations where bodies were waged
for so many pounds of copra, the sweet meat that's compressed to make oil.

In another photograph, Charmian's back turned, her wide pants
swirling in the warm, moist wind as she photographs what's before her:

> a wide beach
> a storm pressing down from the green hills

Make Them Float in Your Mouth
Aboard the Snark, *1906–07*

If you want a story, look for it. Begin
with the idea of seven years. Imagine a boat.

Build it from paper and ideas. Sail it into the hiss
of lava as it enters the sea. When you reach

your first destination ride a 75-pound surfboard
and fail all day. Watch the plantation workers

cleave sweet fruit with machete again and again
until the story you've told yourself begins to stutter and spit—

Go to Molokai on the 4th of July and see for yourself the small girl
who, missing a nose or an arm and covered with sores,

wears sequined clothes and dances. You have to sail on
past empty pockets and bank accounts—

Watch your itinerary dissolve in the water
next to the Australian yacht converted for blackbirding.

See the machete lines carved into the teak door.
You have to lose all of your water and then be blessed with a storm.

You have to endure sores the size of baseballs that seep and cling to your calves
and thighs. You have to go upriver into the luscious green tangle

of unknown until the flowers emerge: red, hibiscus-like,
large enough to contain the whole sunset-syrupy sky.

You have to find that island. Make it float in your mouth.

Bad Penny

She said he was a challenging man
who shone for an audience.
Only way to see him
was to unmask him—kick the audience out
from under his feet; toss him overboard
into a salt-frothed sea and let him blossom—

Away at sea on the small yacht,
she could taste the bitter
transformation. Bring honey,
and bees will swarm and sting.
Everything eye level: body of a shark
harpooned, scooped from the sea
and disemboweled, still snapping air—
And the islands drift in like ellipses,
a pause between each paradise. And from under,
a chronic anger erupting to make more islands.

He was a challenging man—
mind like gasoline set to a flame.
Had she seen his blossoming?
Even as his mind muddied.
Even as the storefront façade
they carried in front of them began to fall apart.

Even as the bitter taste entered her mouth
miles out to sea—

Off Tahiti, December 26, 1907

When the world was rewritten after
     Where are you standing, ghost? What is alive?
months of sea-sway sank you to your skinned knees.
     Yacht scrubbed to shine with bushels of gift limes.
Green-capped mountains rise into blindness.
     Discarded arguments; lies covered in cloud.
As understory pressed up from the jungle's pulse—
     Could things be different? What happens now?
Smoke of reefs beneath, harbor lights beyond.
     If you witness past the self: holdover
Put ear to the dirt—lava pulses underground.

Hands in Your Pockets

Aboard the Dirigo, *1912*

History sings in our faces,
a tiny little nightmare
under moderate but baffling winds
before squalls and rain.

You get your first deep-sea color now.
History keeps singing in our faces.
Indigo, milky, frothed waves
tossed in moderate but baffling winds.

Your first deep-sea color.
What you call Carmel blue
under the white froth of rocking waves
sailing through a circular storm.

Do not feel equal, yet.
Even on waves smooth as Carmel blue,
work itches in your fingertips
like a circular storm.

Wretched night of hive of mind.
Do not feel equal, yet.
Stand with your hands in your pockets,
work itching your fingertips.

Even when we are all going to the bottom.
That wretched night. Mind like rain.
Like a Russian song
catching in the pocket of throat.

At the bottom, a tiny nightmare,
like a man falling from the rig,
like a dog safely tethered to the deck by a string.
Before the squalls and rain

weave into needlework, more than a thread of truth,
because history will sing into our faces.
Like a tiny little nightmare
until our machinery of life resumes.

On Seeing the Red Bird off the Coast of Argentina
Aboard the Dirigo, *1912*

In the time between and the time after,
the air moved like a pampero, cold breath
covering everything. They shortened sails.
Readied for whatever futures might blow in.

First were the mosquitos, those small
machines of fury clouding their heads. No
room free of them. Then,

the wasps came: war of sickle and sting.
They took shelter below deck but couldn't parry
their assault. Pale moon gasping on water.

That's why, when the red Argentinian
bird appeared, no one had words to speak
relief, or there must be land close by, or

after the squall opens the powdery
resolution of the stars.

A Ship Is a Dream in a Snowstorm
Aboard the Dirigo, *1912*

No one can tell you what you can't see under
until you've been under there yourself—

Icebergs, for example, are pristine rising up,
but under hide an ice so old and thick it smells foul as ammonia.

Below, the stove that keeps them warm
totters on the brink. Gas fumes pour into their rooms.

Nothing to do but rise to the surface for air.
Their heads pulsing—

As snow falls, she paces the deck
and marks the dream with the braille of footsteps.

Dwarfed by oilskins and boots. Night inks her orbit.
The crew say, *It hasn't even begun to get cold*—

Snow powders the deck. When she looks up
—between squalls and clouds—
five jewels of the Southern Cross. Sharpen.

Hole in the Sky
Aboard the Dirigo, *1912*

On nights when they search
for mountains of Magellanic Clouds,
the sailors punch holes in the sky.
Coal sacks. Darkness so deep and velvet
it pours back into
the telescopic eye.

By day, she walks the deck
on wet, bare feet.
Sharks circle their ship.
Until one is hooked and hoisted
onto the deck. The men smell blood,
gather to rip its rough belly open.
Pour what's left of it—body and chum—
back into the churning sea.

And somehow it swims on,
crooked, spelling a dark sentence
back into the deep.

What comes are the others. The like-bodied.
The like-minded. Until what was body,
what was sandpaper-skinned and muscle-taut, blooms
into a mountainous cloud. Into deepness.

Instructions for Sailing around Cape Horn, 1912
Aboard the Dirigo, *1912*

Record the miles. Record the hours you sleep
each night. Tell us whether or not you were covered
in bedbugs. *Did they bite?* Describe the bunk, the chart room
where you slept. Record the exact latitude and longitude,
the date. Wish for a smaller boat you could control.
Define the purple depths from their surface. Listen
to the lisp of the captain's phonograph, his rough voice.
Secretly steal his name to stitch into a text. Sew. Type. Write.
Try one thousand words a day. Describe the clouds caught in golden light.
Record your cribbage score when you win. Record the hours
you've slept. The miles you've walked around
the deck. Dream of the ship in warm moonlight.
Sew a new flock of baby clothes from the cloud's light.
Let them flutter away over the wooden rail. Record
the latitude and longitude. Record the date your heart became ballast.
Wish for a smaller boat. Sew. Read *The Red Lily.* Catch an albatross.
Write. Record the miles. Play the ukulele, the moon wet and bedraggled.
Keep those close to you tethered by a string. Look for an escape.

Curse
Aboard the Dirigo, *1912*

What is metaled, what is stretched taut enough?

What's said—*an albatross "happens"*—backlit by white and golden flurries
of clouds.

Can't you see it soaring above the ship?
A sentence of air, lisping
between miles of wire and rope and sails.

O My World she says. To mean that floating island of steel.
To mean the damn bird that circles so often she's trapped in its orbit.
To mean that when the sea is not too loud she can hear his whispers
from the adjacent wooden bunk—

What fate did they shoot out of the sky to hang in imagined rooms?

On the deck, the dead bird, listless, held up by Nakata, becomes almost human.

Lost Bodies
Aboard the Dirigo, *1912*

Days when Charmian spoon-fed the captain egg whites and rubbed his blue
feet, his missing wife hovered in air, a seagull kiting a low wind.
Somehow, he stayed alive until a crown of pines spindled the fog
at the mouth of Elliott Bay and the schooner slid into port at Seattle.

On deck, the doctor's boots sounded like exclamation points.
How the captain's eyes bore into hers: *promise me you'll telegram her.*
While the wife was a continent away in a room where their daughter
nursed a newborn. Sun filtered in, catching motes of dust until they glistened.

After the captain died, night swelled and tossed, a storming sea.
Instead of a telegram, Charmian typed a long letter
chronicling the journey from Baltimore, around Cape Horn.
How Magellanic Clouds piled like mountains on the horizon,

and at night the jewels of the Southern Cross burned in the sky.
How the shark fought to stay alive even after its guts had been spilled on
the deck and the albatross circled the ship. She would write it that night.
She would write it again and again and never be able to shed its weight.

About my neck was hung
Aboard the Dirigo, *1912*

Had they believed in omens, had they known
the way the albatross would stretch over
the cool deep that had seeped into the pools
that kept the thrashing reptiles of their minds sated.

On deck, the bird stood ten, perhaps twelve feet.
Wings, a muscular arc. What filled her head
was her cavernous room still being built
at Wolf House in Glen Ellen—how the bird
might have soared between thick-knuckled rafters.
How she wanted to kill it and did. How
she brought it back. Then, months later, startled
awake by Eliza's screams, by the low
moan of loss from her husband, she looked out at

the ridge where their home had once stood
and remembered that bird; saw its ghost
fly out from the smoke.

Sailor on Horseback

A window can be clear or freckled with air—
can be leaded with the set metal
of an accepted history. In the photo,
he is seated on his horse set against
scalloped golden hills over a braille of
valley farms. The foreground, a sea of untamed
grass. Here, it will always be spring. A day
before the first Japanese lanterns will open their blooms
of seed to chance winds. A day before
oily poppies will punctuate everything
in exclamations. A day before fog
will threaten to shorten the distance—
On that day, there was no one behind to record
Charmian's eye looking into the lens
of her camera to capture his portrait.
Let us set the record straight.

Ghost Oak

Appearances are ghosts. Life, a ghostland—
The towering oak splays its blackened
arteries toward sky, unaware that a pair
of buzzards perch and clot the spiral of tributaries
that wind and unwind toward
whatever blue has arrived in the sky.

How like our own aging bodies the oak
stands, passenger of air and time but blind
as Tiresias. What choice do we have
but to step into this wooden shell and rise?
Shake off the rot the fog brought in because
life lies in order to live. You'll never
know how many dark birds brood in your eaves.

His Elegy

When you hear hoofbeats, think draft horse. Think barns
hewn of unmatched stone. Think silos standing
up against mountains. Think cactus without thorns.
Think oak leaves and the whisper of creek. Think path to a dried-
up pond. Think how cool the water once was.
Think stone rolled over an urn. Think poison oak tall as trees.
Think the ranger who said the Miwok ate
the leaves to cure themselves of the poison.
Think blue ribbon at the California State Fair.
Think from his window he could see fireworks,
too ill to leave the hotel. *How to pass a cure from here to there?*
Think only days left. Kidney stones. Unable to eat.
Think the body gathering what it can't let go.
Think last words. Think Charmian's desperate plea:
Mate, please don't leave me.

November

The day was overcast. Sky held its breath, a defiant child. Mist
clung to Sonoma Mountain in a thin veil. Starlings circled the stone barns

in dizzying shapes. Eucalyptus groves moaned from a light wind;
a few branches clattering to moist and fragrant ground.

The night before, Charmian had looked through the window
from her sleeping porch to his and saw him sleeping peacefully (the first time
in weeks).

She chose not to disturb him. Lay down in her own bed—just a wall of glass,
a bit of air away and slept (the first time in weeks). When she awoke

she was in another world, a day she'd never resolve. He was already gone:
kidneys shut down; body slumped on the floor. They tried—

lifted him, fed him coffee, walked him like a giant stuffed doll. The parade
of doctors ferried in, directing remedies. Until his breath caught in his throat
and stopped.

And since it was November a light rain fell, disrupting the path of birds,
strengthening the earth's fragrant scent that rose up to meet him.

Dark Albums

That putting together the patchwork of photos into the spined order of dark
leather albums was for solace—
>   a tending to the fray that had begun to blur the corners of her
>   mind like a cataract.

White grease pencil notes: ghosts of names, a past we've forgotten the words to.

Some may say: *Let her sleep, heart bundled in briars, mouth sewn shut.*
The dawn staining awake again and again over that mountain that is the
beginning of the world.

Oh, but every sleep has its end and here we are.

The pages that were almost lost to time have awoken again.
Piecing back the story of a life, pixel by pixel

until there she is, Charmian Kittredge London riding astride on her sorrel mare,
dust kicking up, the whole sky above opening like a question—

What the Water Wants

is only to part open what it contains—

    the way the hillside gives,
    the way the ship slides through unknown depths.

After months of nothing comes rain.
Comes sleeplessness. Comes the vision.

    Beacon flashing from the mountainside,
    then, the shadowy body walking down
    toward her home made of stones.

She knew him by his gait, earth opening to his feet.
By how her heart parted its waters to contain the dark dream of him—

    Weeks later, after she had bathed in the lake,
    and ridden the dusty-eyed buses back home,
    she understood what had opened in her that night:

another life.

Smiling into the Ruins of Wolf House

There are the tall trees that blaze in the night:
hungry rockets of blue fire. Then, there is the smoke
that lingers like a question for years to come.
What's left after the great fire are stones:
still blackened and stacked, murmuring moss.

When the photographers come to the ranch,
he's been dead thirty years.
Charmian stands tall, in the doorway where once
they had imagined a door, wearing a sweater
the color of sky. She is smiling at the camera.
She is surrounded by the ruins. You won't know this photo.

This isn't the understory that was left to survive
under the forest that's grown up around this ruin.
It isn't written on placards at the state park.
It has been buried in the innards of a cement building.

Still, there she is at the threshold: not a door, something more.

Something that seeds us as we pass.

The Water Cell Escape

That the heart is not shaped like a trick box,
though velvet-tongued, though bottomed with a spring-
loaded door that opens when pressed enough.

That one can feel sealed in that smooth, fogged glass.
The night she met Houdini the crowd of hundreds
hushed as they watched his daring escape.

That the chains were heavy and marked the skin
and two of the extras disappeared. First,
her sickened husband, then Houdini's young wife.

That the heart is not shaped like a trick box.
Letters folded into tiny stars up
against the milk-star sky of a clear night.

That you have to fold your body just right.
The weeks she spent in New York like chambers
of an ever-turning nautilus shell.

That the water was cold. That it rose fast.
That always at the center of the shell
there was nothing solid to hang on to.

That underwater everything looks and
sounds like a dream. Hair blooms, chains loosen—

That the heart is not shaped like a trick box
and one can walk off that dark stage, alone,
to nothing but the custody of stars.

The House [with] Happy Walls

> *sometimes empty brackets signify a tear or a worn place.*
> —Susan Howe, *Debths*

Between the rafters   weight   of old oak   sunken
to the depth   of memory   purple blue.
[*Took her twenty years to complete the house.*]

Stones carried   stacked cells   form a new creature
hybrid/Hydra   Medusa freed from her cave
[*When a woman raises her head to meet your eyes, she becomes a monster.*]

Each window   lead lined   Fire   and all its possible
stories of erasure   shut out.
[*She was trying to find a secret passage between the life she once had and   *]

Valley   settled   onto golden haunches
Sun rolled   up and down   blue-powdered sky
[*And the life where she'd found herself shipwrecked caught a tide.*]

Fountain speaking water in dining room floor   Stevenson's white dishes
bought from   the woman with the tattooed face.
[*Somehow in the revision they forgot her desk.*]

Calabashes   dim the light of each   fixture
Tapia-cloth curtains   rustle their stories   in the window seats.
[*Walls rose. Story of songbirds gathering in the scrub oaks and bays. Still singing.*]

Disaster on the Mountain

Some mountains you look to daily like calendars.
Are they green or golden-flanked today? Wooded, or stripped bare of trees?

Are they smooth-faced or pocked by deep quarries?
Are they staring back at you clear-eyed or veiled in fog?

She marks her days with these encounters. Even though she knows
the mountain doesn't see her, it centers her in her life.

That's why when the plane carried fourteen passengers into the face
of the San Gabriel Mountains she could not breathe.

Bodies carried down on makeshift stretchers. Deaths reported on the radio.
Only Osa Johnson was (barely) alive. Charmian thought, if Osa survives,

she must teach her how to live as a widow. She pulls the cloak
of the surviving night sky close around her throat.

Grave

There are gates,
once redwood-strong,
we have left to rot
as evidence of our
departure and return.

Wind roars in the trees,
a ravenous sea
when we speak,
shipwrecked from the dead.

The weight of the urn
Charmian carried
the day of his funeral.
How it became heavier
with silence every step
she took closer to the grave.

The first stone barn
lost to our eyes,
folding back into itself.
What remains inside?
A lost stagecoach,
rotting hull of the *Snark?*

We sew together
strangers' voices to find
the story we can't feel
with our hands in this dark.
The seam where what we *know*
welds smoothly into what we *feel*.
A new, steel gate that will not rot.

The phone numbers to the dead
written on a cedar-plank wall
in a closet now empty of a phone.

The desire that opens up
like a mountain view
lost to nearly a century of brush.
And what opens up
when we finally see into it:

    A valley of murmuring air.

Stroke

She was floating in the bath looking at
the ceiling as if it were a constellation of stars

when time shook out its mane. Flung her, dumbstruck,
out to sea, into deep water. So blue

it pressed into purple. Water became tepid.
Can't sail through these doldrums without sail—

After, her writing slanted. Crowded. Tossed
itself overboard. Memory seeped from

the deep, clouds of man-of-war breathing sting—
Until she again became a young girl

wearing a black cashmere dress. Steam hushing
the platform. The weight of her past leaving—

an engine backing away.

House Empty Speaks Loud a Truth, 2018

1. House made of breath exhaled from wooden ribs.

2. Dale Carnegie's name scribbled on a cream closet door.

3. A nautilus shell eating a light bulb sheds the softest light.

4. Calabashes painted gray sway from their ropes whenever the earth shakes. (Someone tried to mute their color.)

5. She designed the house so that it would never burn.

6. The rock patio has a pyramid-shaped staircase that leads up and over the edge.

7. Left unattended, I slid every window latch open, shimmied through sliding doors.

8. You could hear the red-breasted robins singing from the second floor.

9. The silver-painted wallpaper came off on my fingertips.

10. What they thought was a guest room was actually her office.

11. When the state cataloged the house, everyone forgot she was a writer.

12. It never burned.

13. Bays and oaks move closer to the house. (Hear their leaves whisper?)

14. Though they'll cover the fountain in the sun-filled dining room, its waters will keep broadcasting to future visitors.

Box 2: Autobiography

Let go said the
What.
Let go said everything.

—Brenda Hillman

Contents

Description
The uncovered life of Iris Jamahl Dunkle (1974–), a poet, daughter, mother, and resident of Sonoma County, where wildfires burned 36,810 acres in 2017. This destruction reminded Iris of her origins: how her grandmother migrated to California from Oklahoma during the natural disaster of the Dust Bowl.

Places
Freestone
Sebastopol
Santa Rosa
Mendocino
Napa
Sonoma
Tioga Pass
Oklahoma
Hospitals (various)
The sea: Pacific

Documents
Various hospital records
Letters 1984–98
Articles from *The Press Democrat*
Evidence of the Great Fire of 1870
Evidence of the Hanley Fire of 1964
Evidence of the Tubbs Fire of 2017

People
[a series of nested dolls]
Self :: Mother :: Grandmother
[an extraction]

Directions Home after the Firestorms, 2017

1. Follow the ash heaps, the hills arching their black skin.
   History hums like a refrigerator underneath—
   you should have listened, listened.

2. These days the sky—bruise, cloud, sky—opens obscenely;
   look closely enough and you can see up her skirt.

3. Look for the door in the mountain. Steel tooth. Sealed with wax.

4. They say: *spring and all her glory.*
   They say: *the quick and the dead.*
   They say: *bright green stitches will rewrite this landscape.*
   Will we know it?

5. Dump trucks heavy with debris.
   Hawks circle, catching thermals.
   A drone humming on the horizon
   taking pictures of the dead.

6. Will I always be afraid of a warm wind?

Ashes than Dust

A fox sprinted across the dark driveway:
orange spark that trailed through the headlight's spot.

You register this sighting as a charmstone. Then,
drive on into the life you'd written one way,
then revised due to characters disappeared.

In the nightmare. No, in the dream.
There's a dead body, writhing nest
of black and white snakes
rewriting what was lost.

When you wake you would rather
be ashes than dust. You would rather blaze out
like the fox, a fur of sparks in the night,
than be left to rot, be untold.

By now, you thought time would have righted the swerve.
Thought your tires would have found tread. Instead,

you live in an echo chamber where owls
call. And call. And call.

Sunk

Sometimes, the dead speak back to me in the
voice of artifact :: weight of my mother's
gold ring on my middle finger :: comfort ::
When lungs fill with air they should bloom like spring trees ::

The town by the sea was built on bluffs :: logged
redwood forest :: Sea swell sounds like breath should ::
Old stumps were dredged from the river and sold
to the rich tourists as "vintage redwood" ::

The *Vasa* warship stayed sunk in Stockholm's
crystal clear harbor for four centuries ::
before they dredged it up :: built the museum ::
only treasure found aboard :: a gold ring ::

At Big River Beach Mr. Albertson
carved mythical figures out of redwood
stumps :: My mother's been sunk for over a
year :: sometimes she still speaks through the gold ring ::

a replica :: What Mr. Anderson
carved :: Father Time :: Transience Hourglass ::
Acacia Branch :: The Weeping Girl :: Her Hair ::
time rippling over them/me :: the river ::

the clear bay :: Mother, can you dredge me up?

Acceptance Speech, or How to Be a Martyr

Hello. I join you here today from an outcropping of land. From limestone-bedded soil. From salt on wind. From the over-bloom of too much rain. From trying to stay above that throb of earth.

We are born to it. Two feet on the very ground we will be buried in.

Can you smell it? That rot and beauty?

My mother keeps telling me she is dying. She lives a hundred yards away, but she may as well live in my ear. She buzzes like yellow jackets infesting the whole property. She populates and hides in bare stalks like poison oak in winter.

My mother collecting tumors in her belly like eggs.

Can I say now that I'm sinking?

In closing, I want to remind you that good daughters don't want their mothers to die.

In closing, I want to tell you the sky is made of nothing except air and light. Gray as stone. Heavy as all hell.

What did those women think when they walked into that cave and found nothing? No body. Just a message hidden in the wet earth. Pushing up in the buds on the trees. Throbbing. *You must believe in it to tell it.*

In closing, I want to say—

After the Seventh Night of the Northern California Wildfires

For seven nights
there were no stars,
only sky muted

by smoke. First night,
the dry bones
of the past rattled

the eaves of the hillside
of valley oaks. Then, raging,
hot-throated wind stirred,

sparked flames. Until
the mountain cracked open—
A person is most alone

when she looks
at the moon stained red,
at stoked hillsides

shimmering. Every
house a single cell
of the same beast:

fragile and ignitable.

Poem for the Lost Summer

For whatever we lose(like a you or a me)
it's always ourselves we find in the sea
—E. E. Cummings, "maggie and milly and molly and may"

         This was the summer
of erasure: each step we took washed out
from under us. *Have I ever told you*
about the place we love the most? An island
that stutters its own existence, appears
and disappears with each passing tide.
It is a lost manuscript that we can
only read with—

The shells we find there are so small they would only look
right in a dollhouse.

         This is my map made
of sand, my walking into wind until
it carries me, stinging forward into the real chop and surf.
This is my children lost in the fog.
Their voices like—

You, who I could not save, listen to me.

The hills have gone golden, mute with time's pass.
One month. Two. Plath-ing. Little death cave dug
out in my heart, crawled into. At night stars
still explode in their furious milky
fire. *Say stay. Say look up. Say dig out—*

The surgeons say the brain liberated
from the skullcap is beautiful;
Did you bloom in your last hours,

Mother? No one looked under. We only
stood. Vigil. Combing straight hair,
gold as the hills. As you stilled.

Listen to this: I heard your protest.
It dug into me, pulling me

apart. The faint scent
of lavender and rosemary
lingers on the fog.
When the hills green again,
I will try and let you go.

Free to Rise

About the sky, I have some opinions;
Pinpricked utterances that sharpen into
night sky. Had I freedom to rise, I
would hot-air-balloon out of this far-off field—

    What wonders would I see as I rose? Barn,
    field, cursive of trees, roads that shoot out like
    gray meteors. Then, a map that's hedged by
    serpentining river, hunger of sea.
    And me, rising in my crazy orbiting.

Had I not swallowed stones as ballast or
worn the leaden moon boots of grief—
Stitched from the distance and time
that always pull between stars.

Ground Truthing after the Great Fires

When our bodies   were still fogged
with desire   we'd park   in the dark   on the barren gold hills
and look out   at the jeweled city   below us.

We were too young   to remember   the fires
that swept the hillside   clean of oak and scrub.

Now, rattlers slept   under weathered rocks
and barn owls   the size of toddlers
sat like prophets   in the remains of trees
but we couldn't see them.   Our cars clouded   with breath.

When the years   drifted on   and we left   for college
and the hillside   was sold   leveled and built up:
houses rose,   ghosts on the ridge.

We weren't the only ones   who hadn't seen
the remains   of the last fires.

We who returned   woke   from our middle-aged lives
to choke of smoke;   skies pulsing crimson.
Ash, like heavy rain,   drifting down.   The moon
a red eye.   News looping   the same story:
fire that won't stop.   The whole hillside where
we'd once parked,   pressed our bodies against each other,
burned by a fire so hungry   it became a wall   that jumped
the freeway   to find more to burn.

On that windy night   ·   we were all of the same body.
The city   we had once looked out across   was in us.

Forgotten   the Great Fire of 1870.
Forgotten   the Hanley Fire of 1964.

Soon to be forgotten   the Tubbs Fire of 2017?
Even though   the land tells us that all three fires   devoured the same path.

Now when young red-tailed hawks   scream across
the air   above our homes,   when the barn owls
roost   on the eaves of trees,   and the crows
shuffle in the oaks,   we know it is warning
or plea.   *Fire will pour its velvet tongue*
across your valley   again and again,   even if you don't remember.

Artists Speak of the Elements

That the people in the room had all looked in
the river and once seen only themselves
was evident. That was before the smoke
cleared. Now, their minds were like dandelions—
puffs of seed clouds lost and found by the wind.

There was the man who bent steel. The girl who
found treasures buried in ash. Another
who whispered the words of others in charcoal.

The invisible is thick. We agreed.
And when the world in all its forms is on
fire you can't help but find another
element to inhabit in this wind.
Perhaps the world can be after all?
We dreamed in a room made of
scorched earth and believed it could bloom.

Breaking Trail after a Great Fire, Clover Dairy, Sonoma, California

On the hillside—
whose green shag
had been devoured
by hundreds of hungry
goats each spring—

the winds rose,
licked life into sparks
until they became
a red wave: a great storm
of flame and scorch.

The old tin dairy barn
at its base melted into itself
to reveal—after weeks and bulldozers,
clouds of ash—a small, brick door
you'd never seen before.

Each day you drive past
the reconstruction,
you want to open that door
more, even as the hillside
heals: clouds of yellow
mustard and purple lupine;
even as the goats return:
short, stubborn bodies
lost in a sea of rebirth.

You can feel the soft buzz—
darkness singing, hillside
breathing—*don't forget*—
from behind the door.

After the Disaster: Santa Rosa

Weeks after the great 1906 earthquake
destroyed the city, he and Charmian rode
their horses from Glen Ellen into Santa Rosa
to visit Burke's Sanitarium looking for the salve
of utopia: tent cabins set up on a hillside
next to rock-bedded creeks, wind
whispering through fragrant bay leaves.

What they found then was what we see now:
on the surface, blackened hills, a city still smoldering
at its foundations. Charred houses leaning
against the smoke-choked sky—

And though the lumber was scarce
and still sticky with sap, and though
there were too few strong arms to wield hammers,
everything that was lost a century ago was rebuilt.
You see, in this city, again and again, kindness pushes
up from the parched soil like a good crop.

Anniversary

What is time, anyway?   she said, fading
into bruised sky.   Pale Venus.   Sliver moon.
Red din of Mars.   Punctuating distance.

Ground bound.   Can't see you from here.   Fire blooms.
Pomegranate horizons.   Clouds.   Storms.   Sky
mute of stars.   Have to imagine your orbit.
Hope   in another year's time   you'll circle back.

When the fire's out.   When time's pushed on.   Until—
Something wild perches in the dark.   *Is it an owl?*

Weight.   Feathers.   Just out of reach.

Communion of Dust

It's how I arrived in this place. Dust. Blood.
Thin figures. Shadows stretched like bars
against a farm gone fallow. Gone dust. Gone wind.

My grandmother said, *Steinbeck never got it right.*
The place. The leaving and how it felt:
to be child in a world gone back to dust.

She'd breathe the dust into me some birthdays.
Or when I'd come back to visit from college.
Until the dust stuck to my tongue, clouded my eyes
as I tried to drift farther and farther away.

She whispered into my ear the songs she'd sung
in the canneries those long hours she'd worked as a child.
Until the land had become me. No way to escape
the need to carry it, to tell it.

Tioga Pass and My Okie Heritage

The ascent alone could stop a heart. Shale
shards raining down hillsides in a slow slide.
Have I ever told you I can't make
it up a climb that steep? Especially
wearing this dress stitched of gravity and time.
Especially during a superbloom:
all those blue-eyed forget-me-nots staring back.
Especially driving a Model T.
Because the getting there was so dusted,
choked. The land had folded. Everything
packed and loaded, strapped into the back
of the tin car like a lost circus. Because
she was alive when they left Oklahoma.
Because she was a twin: entangled in
another's life in a constrictor knot.
Because her eyes were blue as glacier-melt
lakes. Because what could they have done with her
seven-year-old body once she went deep and cold.

Because I've built my family's stories out
of makeshift shacks. Blankets tacked to walls, flapping
tongues in the wind. Because the granite walls
of the Sierra Nevada mountains
rose to meet them once they made the ascent.
Because she became a blue moth, a barn swallow
sewing the sky shut at twilight,
a constellation that blurred
into the swift current of the Milky
Way. Because I never learned to untie
the knot that held what we'd carried up.
Never learned to dive deep into that want.

Under Campestral Skies

On days when the sky splits like a wide field
about to burst into golden mustard
blossoms; memories push up—rogue bulbs whose
white fists pulse like neurons' electric reach.

When the field of her brain was tilled bare my
grandmother spoke only in verse. Her windows
framed the slow sea. Her voice rose like a moon.

Years sow and turn a field once thick with rye
fallow and pocked with gopher holes. It took
less than an hour for my mother's mind
to lose its moor and drift off. Until she
looked at us with ravenous eyes from a
far meadow we would never find. Deep in
the woods—an exhalation of soft green grass.

And us, left standing under all this sky.

Sinkhole

Driveway washed out. We are done
drifting from place to blown place.

A silver boat lies like a question on
the side of the road. River keeps rising.

It is our heritage to continue through:
dust storm, drought, fire, flood, mudslide, earthquake.

The woods around our house lean in, listening
for what the seasons have to offer up.

When you reroute a river :: restitch a
seam. Something breaks.

My grandmother sat close as her radio
spit hate. Even a small spark can ignite.

When you live this close to a river, this
close to the woods, this close to a fault line,

better know your way out, fast. How will I
pack all her hate? Once saw a river stitched

into the ceiling. Blue and silver sequins
snaking across; as if change could be caught.

This time we will dig out. Our mouths
will be dry, stuffed with feathers.

*

Second time the rain washed our driveway out
the brick-red teeth of the road were revealed.

Is this my inheritance? Owls don't come
out in rain, so the sound of our sentinel is gone.

Red bricks cemented together under
three feet of river rock we've shoveled on.

Once the previous inhabitants came
back to sit with the stone-jawed creek.

They never revealed their source. Or why they'd
hidden statues of Greek goddesses in the walls.

My grandmother could be a low morning
fog that clings to the trembling redwoods.

Or she could be the minerals beneath
soil that stubbornly hold this whole thing down.

Now that the owls have gone mute. Now that
all we built is washing away: gravel, mud,

the weight of what we've been collecting—
My tongue has gone heavy. Too many stones

washing down. Now that the skeleton (blood-
red bricks) has shown its form. Our underneath.

The rain will keep coming whether we live
or die. We will hold our story down.

Box 3: Recorded History

*Americans believed about the West not so much
what was true but what they thought ought to be true.*

—Henry Steele Commager

Contents

Description
"The West" (aka "the last frontier of American settlement") is an imagined area of the United States that can include everything from Oklahoma to California. It is marked by genocide, natural disasters and society that operates just outside the law.

Places
Archives, both seen and unseen, known and unknown
The American West as it was perceived in the 1980s
Mission San Francisco Solano
The Frontier
The Russian River
The San Joaquin Valley
Weedpatch Refugee Camp
Donner Pass
Ancient Rome
The night sky

Documents
Turner's Thesis
California Women: A History
Dances with Wolves
The Revenant
Tibullus, *Book Four*
Palaephatus, *On Unbelievable Tales*

People
[the unspoken]

Archive (a Duet)

Mud, feel of silk. Mind can bloom into
anything, plant it deep enough.
Marigolds loll on lollipop heads.
Wind scatters and bends.
[*since California is its own muse . . .*]

___

Raw-throated. Storm
grows. Loud as years. Hunger,
something you hold in your hips.
[*within pure joy, a kind of hollow*]

Things moving. Anonymity of motion.
Face pressed to glass.
A found light at tunnel's edge.
[*weather is not the window's fault*]

Words shaved by sparks
Danger conserved in the bog of the mind.
What rises, revises surface.
[*oh the bodies I loved were very tired*]

___

At the fair, at every fair, the psychic sits
in a moveable booth behind
skin of lace and fear. Pace sidewalk.
[*I was no sad animal no graveyard*]

___

Night sweats. Sound of owls.
Deconstruction through
a construction of questions.
[*and after your research among the transcripts of the institution*
what gives you immortal life turns out to be the breath of another person]

History of the Indian Wars as Seen from the 1980s

Have you seen the one where the handsome white man (shiny brass buttons, blue wool coat with no holes) comes to the prairie and tames a wild wolf, a girl gone feral? The sun is always shining; skies press down blue. How his white teeth glint as he turns the arm of the coffee grinder for his new native acquaintances (not the face-painted, weapon-yielding Pawnee), a gentler tribe who have put aside his mission (the white pickled egg of a lie he has swallowed as to why he is there) to befriend him. If you listen closely, you can feel the sound of ten thousand wagons rolling toward them. Over that knoll, where the camera never pans, eight skinned buffalo rot in the hot sun.

Under a five-month beard,
the truth quivers.

The Map

The questions are slick. Rainbow
sheen as if—

                       without a map.

Facts are rock.   It's up
to you to find the narrative.

Vesuvial, that red fire can create, or—

Mission San Francisco Solano

The adobe—or what is left of it—
covered in swarms of schoolchildren.

They pour from yellow school buses into
the reconstructed chapel, into the long hall,

where watercolors of decomposing missions
blink back from their own destruction.

They pour into the open plaza, where one lucky kid,
chosen from the crowd, dips a string elbow deep

into a cauldron of melted tallow; dips and dips
until it contains story enough to see, to burn.

Afterwards, their bright voices will catch in the blossoming eaves
of the fruit trees that line the cobbled street

as they run, unaware, past the bare cement slab meant to mark
the names of those who were enslaved.

Only the blossoms, carried by wind,
will drop to their soft and vulnerable knees.

Field Guide to the Lost Species of California

It's the small ones that disappear first:
lavender butterflies that once freckled

the greasewood brush, delicate thistles whose ghosts
still sting. Then, we began to lose what we could gather with our hands:

the kangaroo rat, the white splittail.
Hardly even a meal in that tiny body, but we were hungry

for the dull stare of an empty lake void of any life.
We are the algae that comes, after. The green idea

of want and need. Then, when we settled down
into Missions and tilled the land, what we conquered

were human bodies: sweat, cornmeal, and tallow.
Alta California, established in 1769, a machine of labor

swallowing everything in its path: *a caelo usque ad centrum*
"from the sky to the center of the earth."

Frontier: A Definition

1.

A border is porous　　[slipstream]

We used to swim under
　　river's green skin
　　　　dapple of tree's reach

　　　　　　under water violence
　　　　　　　　is muffled. Current
　　　　　　　　　　never caught us

　　　　　　　　　　　　citizens of the same cool
　　　　　　　　　　　　　　stream, under sun's glare
　　　　　　　　　　　　　　　　weaving with cries of bird in air.

2.

Historically: pistol-fisted　　a band of wasteland　　between　　settled

and primitive　　outpost built　　from clear-cut　　and cleaved bodies.

Lay down the steel sentence.　　On which slides　　[steel] [weight]

A front line　　woven with erased footsteps across　　Natchez Trace—

3. A safety valve lets off steam. Without it. Explosion. A million splinters
that pierce—

4. Wilderness looked back at us. Green teeth. Eyes blinking. We had no
name that suited it.

5.

A border, continuous   [a moving line]

Now the river stops
    its quiet speech
        with stone teeth

            no more threading
                our bodies through
                    its depths and shadows

                        under muffle of water's passage
                            we've lost our common tongue
                                under sandy shoal—

6.

A border is a way of life.

7.

We seek the ocean
    to find the edge
        of ourselves.

            Perhaps waves will
                satiate this churn
                    of desire. Border

                        that time chews.
                            Everything conquerable
                                except ourselves. Lone

                                    fort. Mishap of raw
                                    logs. Secrets stoking
                                    the hearth—

River, Speak

Perhaps the river, if it wanted to speak, would
be deep voiced, gravel drawled. Perhaps it would
be forgiving as the low fog that scarves
the valley redwoods. Our discretions
mutter—light rain whispering leaves. How we
gathered, scraped, took and rerouted gravel
to cover our driveways and roads. Gravel
that was once rough gutted ground down to smooth—

I like to believe the river would speak
like a silver assassin. Loud and full
as a tide-swell, as a muscle of mud, flood
that can swallow a Safeway, a whole town.
That could scream out: *You don't know what you've done*
in a voice made from the entire sea.

Dream-Time History of America

Is clouded by dust is tin rot mended
fenders and ruts that suck tires.   Is heavy
load gone sag.   Is hope printed on fliers.
Is a worn map laid out on a warm dash.
Is suitcases stuffed with what's left. Is chairs
splayed, everything tied on with twine.   Is miles
floating slow.   Is the desert of mute dry
air.   Is steady rise into granite-faced
mountains.   Is the valley planted to its
brim with crops.   Is you may be hungry but
you can't eat what hangs from the vine.   Is barbed
wire rolled out.   Is signs screaming GET OUT.   Is,
finally, a small shack.   Is mud puddles
you look into trying to find the sky.

The Winter of 1846–47

There is a hole in the narrative, dear
reader. Accept. Will you do what
it takes to survive? Or lie down in the deep
drift to let go?

starved, snow-blind. Thirty-three days they walked,
of this winter? What will be on the other side
throb from the frozen Yellow monkeyflowers, Shasta lilies
path that got me here.

What We Left Behind Was Corporeal

Sometimes history is built from thousands
of teeth left in the walls by previous
inhabitants. Sometimes it is written
over in bone. Palaephatus argued
that the ancient women warriors known as
Amazons were likely just men in drag
because how could an army of women
found cities and defeat even greater
armies entirely composed of men?
Luckily, his theory didn't take. Young
girls can still dream of muscled, sword-wielding
sisters. But he is not alone rewriting
what past we see from here. Oftentimes truth
is tucked into walls (like those teeth), hidden
in plain sight. Take Sulpicia, Roman
woman whose poems were neatly written
into Tibullus's book because she
couldn't publish under Roman law. All
but forgotten until some scholar found
her hidden poems. And even then she
was dismissed. Reader, it's our job to look:
find secret passages between then and
now. Insist that there were more voices than
the ones who got to write the story down.
History is a body we breathe life into.

Daphne's Broken Sonnet

Apples are imagining themselves
onto hillsides—pink petals stick out their
tongues from the dark mouths of branches and the
forest canopy ripens overnight
until it pulses like a green heart. Spring
frankensteins us all—softens our cyborg
brains (admit it: you were thinking about what
mysteries your phone will sing out!). While your
body turns like a tree toward the light. Reader,
some days it's just too much: powder-blue sky,
light wind stirring the leaves as if they are
waving, no, beckoning me to root and
join in. How could I not give in? Trying
to find the song that's buried in the soil.

Breaking Trail at Roxborough State Park, Colorado

There are days when life juts out red and raw
as sandstone. Think: *glaciers did it*. Think: *those*
red teeth aren't trying to stain your heart. Here,
the wild reeks of sage and pink blooms. It hums
in the voices of crickets and birdsong.
Unseen snakes spell away in the tall grass.
But still you walk forward toward whatever
vista you came to see. The meadow where
pioneer cabins and their stories fall
in on themselves. Try not to get buried.
Even deer run, longing for home.

Heliacal Rising

Albedo

Darkness was everywhere—I was under
soil as if under water. Seasons drift
in like a fog. See them hang on the far-
off trees? I am good at holding my breath,
even for this duration. But without
air, one loses sense. Time softens, a creek bank
that's slowly been washed out. I forgot my
story of origin—what I've whispered
to myself since I bloomed in full purple
on the sun-facing mountain. Planted, my
bones have become weapons: jag of jawbone,
saber of hip. I'll fight my way out.

Pleiades

Then, one dark night, I rose from the earth
and saw six glowing jewels hovering
on the eaves of the forest.
They looked like doves roosting,
awaiting dawn's pink, syrupy call.

Once their heliacal rising signaled
the beginning of a journey. So, too, I rise
from my grief into catasterism.

Shall we play a game of erasure? How
many times have their stories been retold?
I'd like to believe they were the daughters
of Amazons. Women too strong to stay
rooted to the ground when the gods pursued.
So they became muscles, feathers, and air.

Reintroduction

There is power in the retelling.
Up here, boomeranged in my orbit, time
refocuses, becomes the old friend it
once was. Six strong-bodied sisters are
pulling me up. We flex at the moon. Rain
is our power. Creeks, rivers, seas gather
our strength. Together we can disappear
whole cities in the wake of our mud.
Once I was a wild iris blooming
on a stony slope. Risked boots and their trample.
Now, celestial, my star weaves through the thick
arms of six others. Night falls and we rise.

Box 1

"Listening to the Caryatids on the Palace of Fine Arts": The Palace of Fine Arts was one of eleven palaces created for the 1915 Panama-Pacific Exposition in San Francisco, California. It was set for demolition at the end of the exposition, as was the custom, but was saved thanks to public support.

"The Year He Was Born": The "he" in this poem (and all the others that follow in this section) is Charmian's husband, the American author Jack London. The Corliss Centennial Steam Engine was used to provide electricity at the 1876 World's Fair in Philadelphia. It was considered a symbol of the nation's growth and its turn toward technology.

"Origin Story: Father, 1851–66": Charmian Kittredge London's father was named Willard "Kitt" Kittredge. He was born and raised in Mt. Desert Island, Maine, but traveled to California in search of gold during the gold rush. He became a captain in the Union army and was stationed in Salt Lake City (where he would meet Charmian's mother).

"Origin Story: Mother, 1870": Dayelle "Daisy" Wiley Kittredge was Charmian's mother. She was born in Racine, Wisconsin, and traveled with her family as part of a wagon train to Salt Lake City, Utah (where she met Kitt at a dance at the barracks). She was a writer and published poetry and fiction in national journals. She became ill after the American Hotel, the hotel they were running and living in in Petaluma, California, burned down, and she died when Charmian was only five years old.

"The Curious Incident with the Horse, Charmian, Age 14": Kitt traveled from Los Angeles to San Francisco to attend the 1886 Encampment of the Grand Army of the Republic. When he fell ill, he was brought to Charmian's aunt and uncle's house in Oakland to recover. He died a month later while Charmian was out retrieving his medicine from the doctor. A phaeton carriage is a popular open carriage that was pulled by one to two horses.

"Truth Walks the Plank, San Francisco, 1890–1900": Charmian destroyed many of her diaries from this era in reaction to Irving Stone, who had accessed the diaries without her consent to write a sensationalized, fictional biography about her and Jack. Charmian worked in San Francisco as a stenographer and commuted daily on the ferry across San Francisco Bay.

"Artifact": King Vasa's ship was built between 1626 and 1628 and sank on her maiden voyage on August 10, 1628. The ship, which was recovered completely intact in 1961, is now located in the Vasa Museum in the Royal National City Park in Stockholm.

"Girl with a Gun Goes Anyway, Malaita, 1909": Jack and Charmian London built a small yacht they named the *Snark*, after Lewis Carroll's poem, and sailed around the South Seas from April 23, 1907, to April 8, 1909, when they had to abruptly end their anticipated seven-year journey due to poor health. Most media outlets found it shocking that a woman would travel in this manner. Blackbirding is the kidnapping and subsequent enslavement of Pacific Islanders, often in countries far from their native lands.

"Make Them Float in Your Mouth": The Londons' first stop on their *Snark* journey was the Hawaiian Islands. They spent time on Molokai, then a leper colony, and also learned how to surf on a 75-pound wooden surfboard.

"Hands in Your Pockets": Jack and Charmian London arranged for passage on the *Dirigo*, which sailed from Baltimore Harbor on March 2, 1912, and rounded Cape Horn to arrive in Seattle on August 12, 1912. Charmian recorded the journey in many different ways: in her personal diaries; in the letter she composed and typed for Captain Chapman's widow shortly after reaching Seattle in August; in the typed version of the diaries she composed on the *Dirigo* and revised after Jack's death; in her chapter "Cape Horn Voyage" in *The Book of Jack London*; in her short letter to the editor of the *San Francisco Chronicle*, titled "Mrs. Jack London recalls her voyage of the *Dirigo*"; and in the chapter "Lean Yankee Aristocrat," about Captain Chapman in Hennessy's *Sewall Ships of Steel* (1937). On the ship, Charmian wrote her first short story, "The Wheel," and began working on "Us," a biography/autobiography that the couple had discussed when Jack had become ill in the Solomon Islands. This project evolved into *The Book of Jack London*. She also collaborated with Jack on several of his onboard writing projects, including *The Valley of the Moon, John Barleycorn,* and *The Mutiny of the Elsinore.* Some of the lines in this poem are from Charmian's typed diaries.

"On Seeing the Red Bird off the Coast of Argentina": A pampero is a strong, cold, southwesterly wind that blows from the Andes across the pampas toward the Atlantic.

"Hole in the Sky": Magellanic Clouds are two irregular dwarf galaxies visible in the Southern Celestial Hemisphere that look like mountains. Coalsacks are what sailors called the Coalsack nebula, an interstellar cloud that is so dense that it obscures the stars behind it.

"*About my neck was hung*": The title of this poem is from a line in Samuel Taylor Coleridge's poem "The Rime of the Ancient Mariner." Wolf House is the mansion Jack and Charmian built on their property in Glen Ellen, California. Sadly, it burned to the ground just weeks before they were to move in.

"Sailor on Horseback": The photograph described in this poem is currently featured on all of the trash cans at Jack London State Historic Park in Glen Ellen, California.

"Dark Albums": Charmian Kittredge London put together dozens of photograph albums. These can be found in the Jack London Papers at the Henry E. Huntington Library in San Marino, California.

"Smiling into the Ruins of Wolf House": The young photographers Hansel Mieth and Otto Hagel visited Charmian at her home, the House of Happy Walls, in the 1940s. They'd recently purchased a nearby ranch and arranged to visit and photograph Charmian because they had long admired Jack and Charmian's work. When they arrived, Charmian took the couple on her sacred walk to the hillside where Jack was buried and the nearby ruins of Wolf House. Photos from that day show Charmian posed in the ruins of Wolf House, dressed in her rugged riding clothes, a wide smile spread across her face. She looks content, as if she is smiling into the beautiful ruins of her life.

"The Water Cell Escape": Charmian Kittredge London first met Harry Houdini and his wife in 1915, when she and Jack attended his show in Oakland, California. After Jack's death, Charmian visited Houdini in New York when she traveled there on business. They had a short affair beginning January 17, 1918.

"The House [with] Happy Walls": Charmian Kittredge London referred to the home she built for herself after her husband died as "The House with Happy Walls."

"Disaster on the Mountain": Osa and Martin Johnson were very close friends of the Londons. The Londons first met Martin when he was hired as part of the crew of the *Snark*. After Martin married Osa, Charmian and Osa became good friends. Martin and Osa became celebrities for their documentaries about their travels. On the morning of January 12, 1937, Martin and Osa, who were on a national speaking tour, boarded a flight bound for Las Vegas and Burbank. The plane crashed near Los Pinetos Peak in California. Martin died the following day.

"Stroke": Charmian Kittredge London suffered a stroke while taking a bath in 1944.

"House Empty Speaks Loud a Truth, 2018": When the House of Happy Walls was being remodeled, I got the opportunity to walk through the structure when it was completely empty. This poem catalogs some of the treasures I found in the empty museum.

Box 2

"Directions Home after the Firestorms, 2017": The firestorms in this poem began on the warm and windy night of October 8, 2017, and continued to burn out of control for three weeks, the worst firestorms in Sonoma

County history. Together the Nuns, Tubbs, and Pocket Fires burned over 110,700 acres in Sonoma and Napa counties.

"Ashes than Dust": A charmstone is an oblong or rounded stone about two to three inches long used by medicine people in Coast Miwok and Southern Pomo nations to extract illness. The stones were thought to absorb whatever ills were extracted.

"Sunk": In 1865, Erick Albertson spent seven years carving the Masonic statue that sits on top of the Masonic Hall in Mendocino, California. The statue is made up of Masonic symbols that mean time, patience, and perseverance will accomplish all things.

"You, who I could not save, listen to me.": The title of this poem is from "Letter Beginning with Two Lines," by Czesław Miłosz, translated by Matthew Olzmann.

"Ground Truthing after the Great Fires": This poem is set in the Fountain Grove area of Santa Rosa, California, which was devasted by the Tubbs Fire in 2017, the Hanley Fire of 1964, and the Great Fire of 1870.

"Artists Speak of the Elements": This poem was written about a meeting of artists at the Sonoma Valley Museum of Art shortly after the wildfires in 2017. The line "the invisible is thick" is from Brenda Hillman's "The Rosewood Clauses," in *Extra Hidden Life, among the Days*.

"After the Disaster: Santa Rosa": The "he" in this poem is Jack London. The 1906 earthquake completely destroyed the town of Santa Rosa. Charmian Kittredge London recorded in her diary a few weeks later that the destruction was so complete, she cried while riding her horse through town. Burke's Sanitarium was a retreat located on Mark West Springs Road, about a mile from Old Redwood Highway in Santa Rosa. In the late 1800s and early 1900s, people would travel there to live in tent cabins and receive restorative treatments.

"Communion of Dust": When my grandmother was a child, she came with her family to California to escape the Dust Bowl. When she said, *Steinbeck* *never got it right,* she was referring to the fact that John Steinbeck set his Pulitzer Prize–winning novel in counties where the Dust Bowl had not occurred and that the characters he created in his novel were not people my grandmother identified with.

"Tioga Pass and My Okie Heritage": Tioga Pass is a mountain pass in the Sierra Nevada range that marks an entrance to Yosemite National Park.

Box 3

"Archive (a Duet)": The italicized lines are from several of Brenda Hillman's poems in *Loose Sugar*. *"[W]ithin pure joy, a kind of hollow"* is from "Arroyo." *"Oh the bodies I loved were very tired"* and *"I was no sad animal no graveyard"* are from "Male Nipples." *"[A]nd after your research among the transcripts of the institution what gives you immortal life turns out to be the breath of another person"* is from "The Mysteries."

"History of the Indian Wars as Seen from the 1980s": The two movies referenced in this poem are *Dances with Wolves* (1990) and *The Revenant* (2015).

"Mission San Francisco Solano": The mission San Francisco Solano is in Sonoma, California. Many of the enslaved Coast Miwok and Pomo people who died there were buried in an unmarked grave; recently, however, a monument has been erected to mark the site.

"Field Guide to the Lost Species of California": Alta California was the original name for the province of New Spain (1769), where the state of California is currently located. After the Mexican War of Independence, Alta California became part of Mexico but was ceded to the United States in 1848 with the signing of the Treaty of Guadalupe Hidalgo. The "machine of labor" this poem refers to is the mission system that was run by the labor of enslaved native people.

"Frontier: A Definition": According to historian and author Greg Grandin, the Natchez Trace was an ancient Native American "road that ran alongside the Mississippi, connecting Nashville to Natchez." The trail marked the line of the frontier for some time.

"River, Speak": Since the 1940s the gravel industry has mined millions of tons of gravel from the Russian River, and this practice is thought to have decimated the salmon population.

"Dream-Time History of America": The Dust Bowl that struck midwestern states like Oklahoma, Texas, and Kansas sent hundreds of thousands of refugees to California to find work. Work was scarce, however, during the Great Depression, and the "Okies" were met with prejudice by local Californians.

"The Winter of 1846–47": The title of this poem comes from the dates that the Donner Party, the pioneer families, who were snowed in in the High Sierras, spent isolated.

"What We Left Behind Was Corporeal": Sulpicia is the author of several poems once attributed to the ancient Roman poet Tibullus.

"Heliacal Rising": The title of this poem refers to the rising of a celestial object when it first becomes visible after a period of invisibility due to conjunction with the sun. "Albedo" is the proportion of light or radiation that is reflected by a surface of a planet. Pleiades is a group of stars named after the seven daughters of Atlas: Maia, Electra, Taygete, Celaeno, Alcyone, Sterope, and Merope. Catasterism is the transformation of a person into a star or constellation after death. Reintroduction is the act of putting a species of animal or plant back into its former habitat.

Acknowledgments

I would like to thank the editors of the following publications, where these poems first appeared, sometimes under different titles and in slightly different forms.

Catamaran: "Hands in Your Pockets" and "Girl with a Gun Goes Anyway, Malaita, 1909"

Construction: "Heliacal Rising"

Cordella: "Sinkhole"

Cranog: "On Seeing the Red Bird off the Coast of Argentina"

Curator Magazine: "River, Speak"

East Bay Poetry Review: "Grave"

Ethel: "The Curious Incident with the Horse, Charmian, Age 14"

Glint Literary Journal: "Ghost Oak," "Dark Albums," and "Disaster on the Mountain"

Green Mountain Review: "Curse" and "Artifact"

Healdsburg Literary Guild Chapbook: "His Elegy"

Helen Literary Magazine: "Stroke"

The Jack London Society Newsletter: "November"

Los Angeles Review of Books: "The Winter of 1846–47"

Mom Egg Review: "Acceptance Speech, or How to Be a Martyr"

Okay Donkey: "Ashes than Dust"

Panoply, a Literary Zine: "Make Them Float in Your Mouth"

Parks and Points: "Breaking Trail at Roxborough State Park, Colorado"

Peauxdunque: "Smiling into the Ruins of Wolf House"

Phoenix: Out of Silence . . . and then, Redwood Writers 2018 Poetry Anthology: "After the Seventh Night of the Northern California Wildfires," "Poem for the Lost Summer," "Communion of Dust," and "*You, who I could not save, listen to me.*"

Pleiades: "*About my neck was hung*"

Poem-a-day, Academy of American Poets: "House Empty Speaks a Loud Truth, 2018"

Postcard Poems: "Mission San Francisco Solano" and "Sailor on Horseback"

Redheaded Stepchild: "Directions Home after the Firestorms, 2017"

Rise Up Review: "Poem for the Lost Summer"

San Diego Reader: "Communion of Dust," "The Map," and "After the Seventh Night of the Northern California Wildfires"

South Florida Poetry Journal: "The House [with] Happy Walls," "Under Campestral Skies," and "*You, who I could not save, listen to me.*"

Split Rock Review: "Ground Truthing after the Great Fires"

SWWIM Every Day: "Daphne's Broken Sonnet" and "Communion of Dust"

Talking Writing Magazine: "Free to Rise" and "Frontier: A Definition"

Taos Journal of Poetry: "Archive (a Duet)"

THAT Literary Review: "Make Them Float in Your Mouth"

Tin House: "History of the Indian Wars as Seen from the 1980s" and "Field Guide to the Lost Species of California"

West Trestle Review: "Sweatshop, Oakland, 1911" and "Truth Walks the Plank, San Francisco, 1890–1900"

Whale Road Review: "Tioga Pass and My Okie Heritage"

Woven Tale Press: "Artists Speak of the Elements"

300 Days of Sun: "The Year He Was Born"

580 Split: "Hole in the Sky"

Displayed as part of the *An Eye for Adventure: Photographs by Jack London* exhibit at Sonoma Valley Museum of Art, January–March 2018: "Make Them Float in Your Mouth" and "After the Disaster: Santa Rosa"

Displayed as part of *From Fire, Love Rises: Stories Shared from the Artist Community,* Sonoma Valley Museum of Art, September 29, 2018–January 6, 2019: "Artists Speak of the Elements" and "Directions Home after the Firestorms, 2017"

Displayed as a part of *Reverberations,* an exhibition at Sebastopol Center for the Arts, October 25–December 2, "Breaking Trail after a Great Fire, Clover Dairy, Sonoma, California" written off of and shown with Picasso's "Tête de Chèvre de Profil"

Displayed on one hundred buses as part of the San Francisco Beautiful and Poetry Society of America Muni Art 2020 campaign: "Listening to the Caryatids on the Palace of Fine Arts"

Awarded first place, Northern California Women's Music Festival Poetry Contest: "Instructions for Sailing around Cape Horn, 1912"

Finalist for the *Don't Talk to Me About Love* 2017 Poetry Contest: "The Water Cell Escape"

* * *

This book was a long journey, and many helped me as it came into being. Of course, first and foremost are my family: Matt, Jack, and Max, who listen to the words when they are brand-new and give me space to make my art. And my father, who taught me how to look deeply and see what is difficult to see.

Several years ago, after reading an early draft of this manuscript, I was lucky to receive sage advice from my dear friend and mentor, Jane Mead: *Hold your horses. Sometimes you have to wait until the book is ready to be finished.* I took her advice, and because of it this book became so much more than it once was.

Then, last summer, Forrest Gander helped me crack open the manuscript and find its true form, and for this I will always be grateful.

Thank you to Kazim Ali for believing in this book.

Thank you to Stephanie G'Schwind for believing in this book and for her incredible editorial skills, which have made it even better than I could imagine. Thank you also to the team at the Center for Literary Publishing— Hannah Barnhart, Annmarie Delfino, Jordan Osborne, and Jess Turner— whose hard work made this book shine.

At the heart of this book is another. I wrote many of these poems while studying the archives at the Huntington Library, UC Berkeley, Utah State, Sonoma County History and Genealogy Library, and Jack London State Historic Park as I wrote the first full-length biography on Charmian Kittredge London. I'm indebted to these collections and their incredible research librarians who helped me navigate their collections. I'm also grateful to the Jack London Society for their support.

I was lucky to find the poetry of Brenda Hillman when I was in graduate school at New York University in the 1990s, then later to get to know her as I worked with her at the Napa Valley Writers' Conference. Thank you for your inspiration and friendship and for helping me navigate the grief of losing my mother.

Thank you to the staff and faculty of the Napa Valley Writers' Conference (Andrea, Angela, Nan, Catherine, Lakin, and Charlotte) for the inspiration you feed me each summer. Thank you, Jane Hirshfield and Camille Dungy, especially for your help with several of the poems in this collection.

Thank you, Jane Shore and Howard Norman, for your continued support, and Jean Valentine for always being an editorial voice in my head so many years after NYU.

I'm thankful to Vermont Studio Center for giving me the time and space to work on these poems and to Rosanna Warren for her keen insight into early drafts of poems.

Nicole Callihan, thank you for your friendship and editorial insight, and to the rest of the Monday poetry group: Sanj, Zoë, Mara, Kat, Ruth, and Caitlin, thank you!

Thank you, Adair, Nicole, Kat, and Amber.

Thank you to the Sebastopol Center for the Arts, the Sonoma County Museum, and the Sonoma Valley Museum of Art, whose support, especially while I was Poet Laureate of Sonoma County, brought many of these works to life.

Thank you to my mother, who taught me to look back and question the past.

This book is set in Sabon
by the Center for Literary Publishing
at Colorado State University.

Copyediting by Annmarie Delfino.
Proofreading by Hannah Barnhart.
Book design and typesetting by Jess Turner.
Cover design by Jordan Osborne.
Cover art by Erika Osborne.